Fasting & Praying WILL Change Your LIFE

JACKIE JONES

FASTING & PRAYING WILL CHANGE YOUR LIFE

Copyright © 2016 by Jackie Jones
JackieJonesMinistries.org

ISBN-13: 978-0-9994911-0-2

Published by: TRAINING FOR THE KINGDOM
New York, NY
www.TrainingForTheKingdom.com

All Rights Reserved. No part of this book may be reproduced or transmitted in any form or by any means, electronic or mechanical, including photocopying, recording, or by an information storage and retrieval system - except by a reviewer who may quote brief passages in a review to be printed in a magazine or newspaper - without permission in writing from the publisher.

Printed in the United States of America

Unless otherwise indicated, all Scripture quotations are taken from the New King James Version®. Copyright © 1982 by Thomas Nelson. Used by permission. All rights reserved.

Cover Design and Layout: Training For the Kingdom

ACKNOWLEDGEMENTS

I would like to dedicate this book to the Holy Spirit. Thank You, Holy Spirit for Your love, guidance and peace that You provide to me each day. I could not imagine life without You. Thank You for teaching me the power of prayer and fasting and allowing me to share it with others.

TABLE OF CONTENTS

How to use this book 1
Introduction 3
Chapter 1 — What is Spiritual Fasting? 5
    Why Fast 6
    Praying While Fasting 8
Chapter 2 — Fasting and Praying Throughout the Bible 9
    The Esther Fast 9
    The Ezra Fast 11
    The 1 Samuel Fast 13
    The Joel Fast 15
    The Jonah Fast 16
    The Fast of Cornelius 18
    The Fast of Anna the Prophetess 20
    The Fast of Isaiah 22
    The Daniel Fast 24
    Jesus Fasted 26
CHAPTER 3 — So Why Fast and Pray 29
Chapter 4 — The Power of Praying the Word of God 33
Chapter 5 — Praying and Believing 41
ABOUT THE AUTHOR 47

HOW TO USE THIS BOOK

1) Find a quiet area where you can commune with God without interruption and distractions.

2) Soft worship music can help set the atmosphere for meditation and worship. I recommend soaking music.

3) Talk to God about your intent to fast and seek His wisdom as to how long and whether to fast a meal or all day. Use wisdom when fasting, especially if you are under a doctor's care. Check with your doctor, remember God also uses doctors to bring forth healing.

4) Read the scriptures outlined in chapter 2 and meditate on them as you fast. Use the prayers as starting points and then continue to personalize your prayer to fit your desires and needs.

5) As you are fasting, set aside time to pray. If you are fasting during your normal breakfast, lunch or dinner time, pray in its place. It may be difficult at first, but keep praying; you will begin to experience the benefits of fasting and praying. When you see the results of fasting and praying, it will soon become a part of your lifestyle.

INTRODUCTION

Please know that if you are reading this book, it is because I love you. I do not have to know you, but the love of God that lives within me, allows me to love my brothers and sisters without ever meeting them. Therefore, I desire to see you blessed and overflowing with the supernatural favor of almighty God. Fasting and Praying can and will change your life. It is my prayer that you receive wisdom, understanding and a desire to fast, pray and spend time with God.

My people are destroyed for lack of knowledge. Because you have rejected knowledge, I also will reject you from being priest for Me; Because you have forgotten the law of your God, I also will forget your children **Hosea 4:6**. The prophet Hosea is reminding us that those who walk blindly will perish! **Knowledge is power!**

The Apostle Paul wrote to Timothy, and I am sharing this with you. *Study to show yourself approved unto God, a workman that need not to be ashamed, rightly dividing the word of truth* **2 Timothy 2:15, KJV**. We should all set a goal to be an approved workman. An approved workman is one who diligently studies the word of God and seeks after the truth! We have a responsibility to read the Bible and live according to the word of God. God gave us an instruction book. In this book we not only learn who God is, but we learn who we are!

I hate to say it this way, but we have become lazy and or too busy. It takes work to study. It takes work to read. It takes work to pray and it takes work to fast. I pray that I can convince you that with a little work and time, you will realize that praying and fasting can change your life and your situation. It will be worth your time and effort!

The depiction of the world as played out in politics, television and social media is one of chaos! Now more than ever, it is pertinent that we study, gain knowledge and open our hearts to hear directly from God!

Fasting and praying will certainly create an atmosphere where you can hear God and receive direction. Through this discipline we become more sensitive to the Holy Spirit! Fasting and praying will open the heavens!

Chapter 1
WHAT IS SPIRITUAL FASTING?

According to Unger's Bible Dictionary the Greek word for fast is "***nesteuo***", which means, "*to abstain*". It means to go without! The book of Esther expounds on this meaning as to abstain from food and drink (*Esther 4:16*). The Hebrew word for fasting is "***tsom***", which literally means, "*not to eat*". Some people may fast television, social media and other desires that they may choose to abstain from for a period of time. However throughout the Old and New Testaments there are examples of fasting with regards to the abstaining from food. This is the fasting that I will be referring too.

Fasting is putting the flesh into submission. Fasting will not allow the flesh to rule in your life. It is a call to turn away from food and seek God. Fasting will strengthen your spirit so that you can stay focused on hearing and serving God.

Fasting is a spiritual discipline that is mentioned throughout the Bible and incorporated by the many great characters in the Bible. It is an intentional decision to abstain from eating. There are various types of fasts described throughout the Bible. I will share some of the different fasts in the next chapter. But first, it is important that you understand why the need to fast is so important.

WHY FAST

Jesus Himself stated in the book of Matthew 6:16-18

¹⁶Whenever you fast, do not put on a gloomy face as the hypocrites do, for they neglect their appearance so that they will be noticed by men when they are fasting. Truly I say to you, they have their reward in full. ¹⁷But you, when you fast, anoint your head and wash your face, ¹⁸so that your fasting will not be noticed by men, but by your Father who is in secret; and your Father who sees what is done in secret will reward you.

Please pay close attention to the word "***when***" in this scripture. Fasting is not mandated but recognized and an expected discipline. Fasting should be a part of your lifestyle. It is a period of time when we deny ourselves the pleasure of food and seek God's face and presence. If you desire a breakthrough, fast and pray. If you desire God's direction, fast and pray. If you desire a closer walk with God, fast and pray. I assure you that fasting and praying will open up your spirit to hear and see your life from a new set of lenses.

I fasted for the purpose of writing this book. I wanted to give you first-hand experience of the benefits of fasting. Before beginning a fast, it is important to seek the Holy Spirit. The Spirit will guide you as to the specifics of your fast. During my first fast, I abstained from food from sun up, to sun down for 3 days. I then ventured on and would fast a meal a day and or would skip a meal. On another occasion I abstained from meat and sweets following the Daniel Fast.

I will explain the Daniel Fast in the next chapter. There is no written script as to how or how long to fast. That is why I said to seek the Spirit for guidance.

During my fast, I became sensitive to the Holy Spirit and the world around me. My eyes were opened and I experienced a clearer understanding of myself and who I am in the Kingdom of God. As I prayed throughout my fast, I felt closer to God and more sensitive to God's voice. I conversed with God daily and received direction and clarity. Although I walk with God daily, the connection during my time of fasting was amazing. I was caught up onto another dimension. My discernment increased. I became more aware and in tune with my body, my breathing and my heartbeat. My knowledge of the spiritual realm increased and the power of God's love was ever so present in every conversation. The gift of prophecy flowed freely as I heard and recognized God's voice. God's presence was indescribable. Fasting has become a part of my lifestyle and it has changed my life. I can't believe that I have missed out on so many years of not understanding the benefits of fasting. However, I am glad that I know now and want to share this with all of you. Fasting will change your life. God will speak directly to you and your situation. Don't sleep on this message, fast and pray. It will change your life. I assure you that miracles will happen when you fast.

PRAYING WHILE FASTING

Praying and reading the word of God is essential during your fast. Especially during those moments of feeling hungry; read the Bible and pray to God for strength. This is your time to commune with God. Put God first and deny the cravings of the flesh. Pray and converse with God. God will speak to you and the word of God will come alive in your heart. Pray the promises of God. We are informed in Joshua 1:8, *"This book of the law shall not depart from our mouth, but you shall mediate in it day and night, that you may observe to do according to all that is written in it. For then you will make your way prosperous and then you will have good success"*. Meditating on the word of God day and night will give you good success and prosperity. Combine fasting, praying and meditating and you will be an unstoppable force in the Kingdom of God!

CHAPTER 2
FASTING AND PRAYING THROUGHOUT THE BIBLE

THE ESTHER FAST

Esther 4:15-17

[15]Then Esther told them to reply to Mordecai: [16]"Go, gather all the Jews who are present in Shushan, and fast for me; neither eat nor drink for three days, night or day. My maids and I will fast likewise, and so I will go to the king, which is against the law; and if I perish, I perish!" [17]So Mordecai went his way and did according to all that Esther commanded him.

Esther fasted for the safety of her family and the Jewish people. Her cousin Mordecai informed her that the Jewish people were to be killed because of the hatred of a man called Haman. Haman did not like Mordecai and the Jewish people. Esther the Queen was also Jewish and upon hearing of the news knew that she had to go before the king to petition for her people. It was understood that no one was allowed to go before the king without an invitation, not even the Queen. Going before the king without an invitation can cost you your life. Esther then called all of the Jews to join her for a fast without food and drink for 3 days.

Esther was accepted into the presence of the king and the Jewish people were saved and Haman was the one executed! You can fast for the safety, protection and salvation of your family! Esther did, and the Jewish people were saved and the enemy was destroyed! Fasting will change your life and the life of those you love.

PRAYER

Lord, I am thankful for Your love, favor and protection. Keep me within Your bosom and under Your wing. Keep Your hand of mercy and grace upon me. Cover my family. Protect them from the hand of the enemy. No weapon formed against us shall prosper. Just like Esther, may we walk in Your presence daily and experience the peace and salvation of God.

Personal Prayer

_____

_____

_____

_____

_____

_____

_____

_____

_____

THE EZRA FAST

Ezra 8:21-23

> [21]*Then I proclaimed a fast there at the river of Ahava, that we might humble ourselves before our God, to seek from Him the right way for us and our little ones and all our possessions.* [22]*For I was ashamed to request of the king an escort of soldiers and horseman to help us against the enemy on the road, because we had spoken to the king, saying, "The hand of our God is upon all those for good who seek Him, but His power and His wrath are against all those who forsake Him."* [23]*So we fasted and entreated our God for this, and He answered our prayer.*

Ezra tells the story of the Jews returning to Jerusalem from captivity in Babylon. Ezra was concerned for the safety of the Jews and their possessions on their journey. He proclaimed a corporate fast asking God for protection over their children and finances. Verse 23 depicts the power of prayer and fasting as it highlights that after the fast, God answered their prayer!

PRAYER

Lord, protect my finances. Open up the door of financial blessings upon my family and myself. Extend financial prosperity from generation to generation. Open up the portals of heaven over my household that we may walk in financial prosperity and protection. I am standing on the word of God believing that

whatever, I ask in the name of Jesus, it shall be provided and come to pass. I believe God for a financial miracle!

Personal Prayer

THE 1 SAMUEL FAST

1 Samuel 7:5-9

⁵*And Samuel said, "Gather all Israel to Mizpah and I will pray to the Lord for you." ⁶So they gathered together at Mizpah, drew water, and poured it out before the Lord. And they fasted that day and said there, "We have sinned against the Lord." And Samuel judged the children of Israel at Mizpah. ⁷Now when the Philistines heard that the children of Israel gathered together at Mizpah, the lords of the Philistines went up against Israel. And when the children of Israel heard of it, they were afraid of the Philistines. ⁸So the children of Israel said to Samuel, Do not cease to cry out to the Lord our God for us, that He may save us from the hand of the Philistines. ⁹And Samuel took a suckling lamb and offered it as a whole burnt offering to the Lord. Then Samuel cried out to the Lord of Israel, and the Lord answered him.*

The Israelites were living in bondage and sin. They needed deliverance and wanted forgiveness. Samuel gathered them together for a corporate fast for deliverance and for them to seek God. The Philistines were ready to attack the Israelites. But God! He caused a loud thunder that confused the Philistines and the men of Israel then pursued the Philistines chasing them out of Mizpah and far away. There is power in fasting and praying. I am telling you, fasting and spending time praying to God will change your life and your situation. If you need deliverance and want to draw closer to God, the answer is to fast and pray. God will confuse the enemy and make the enemy your footstool.

PRAYER

Lord, please have mercy upon me and forgive me for my sins, I do repent and I am sorry for the things I have said, thought and neglected to do. Please wash me in Your blood and clean me from my iniquity. I ask for deliverance from the things I have done and for not following Your word. Please Father, forgive me! I desire to walk upright and according to Your will and purpose for my life. Keep Your hand upon me and all evil away from me. May Your love and mercy saturate me and keep me in perfect peace.

Personal Prayer

THE JOEL FAST

Joel 2:12

¹²"Now, therefore, says the Lord, "Turn to Me with all your heart, With fasting, with weeping, and with mourning."

Again, we learn that fasting and praying opens your heart for repentance and can put you back in relationship with God!

PRAYER

I repent this day of all of my wrong doings. Forgive me for my attitude, my insincere thoughts, my hypocrisy, my pride and my sin. I desire to be more like You Father. Give me a clean heart. I desire to serve You with all of my heart and all of my soul. I will follow Your word and will for my life.

Personal Prayer

THE JONAH FAST

Jonah 3:5-10

⁵So the people of Nineveh believed God, proclaimed a fast, and put on sackcloth, from the greatest to the least of them. ⁶Then word came to the king of Nineveh; and he arose from his throne and laid aside his robe, covered himself with sackcloth and sat in ashes. ⁷And he caused it to be proclaimed and published throughout Nineveh by the decree of the king and his nobles, saying, Let neither man nor beast, herd nor flock, taste anything; do not let them eat, or drink water. ⁸But let man and beast be covered with sackcloth and cry mightily to God; yes, let every one turn from his evil way and from the violence that is in his hands. ⁹Who can tell if God will turn and relent, and turn away from His fierce anger, so that we may not perish? ¹⁰Then God saw their works that they turned from their evil way; and God relented from the disaster that He had said He would bring upon them, and He did not do it.

After Jonah was saved and released from the belly of the whale, God asked Jonah a second time to go to the city of Nineveh and warn them of God's coming judgment. Jonah proclaimed that in 40 days the city would be overthrown. The king and the people of Nineveh believed God and a fast was called. God saw their hearts and did not destroy the city.

Fast and pray and turn from your wicked ways and God will forgive you. Fasting will humble you and crucify the flesh so that you will walk in the truth and recognize your faults.

PRAYER

Lord, show me my areas of sin. Show me my faults, so that I will turn from my wicked ways and repent. Reveal to me those areas of un-forgiveness in my life. I repent now and ask Your mercy. Forgive me for ignoring Your warnings and living carelessly. I desire to walk closer to You and live according to Your will and purpose for my life! I love You Father, surround me with Your love and mercy.

Personal Prayer

_____

_____

_____

_____

_____

_____

_____

_____

THE FAST OF CORNELIUS

Acts 10:30-31

*So Cornelius said, "Four days ago I was fasting until this hour; and at the ninth hour I prayed in my house, and behold, a man stood before me in bright clothing, *[31]*And said, Cornelius, your prayer has been heard, and your alms are remembered in the sight of God.*

God will answer prayer through your fasting and praying. Cornelius had a visitation that directed his next step and confirmed that his prayers were heard. Expect the supernatural move of God when you fast and pray! Expect to hear the voice of God when you fast and pray! Expect to see your prayers answered when you fast and pray! Expect a miracle when you fast and pray!

PRAYER

Lord, I need direction. Help me to make the right decision. I need Your help. Send forth Your ministering angels to guide me. I need clarity in my life. Holy Spirit direct my path. I fast and pray for revelation knowledge. I ask and seek Godly wisdom and step-by-step strategies to combat the enemy and fulfill my destiny. Open up my spiritual eyes, so that I will see clearly and follow Your will and purpose for my life. Open up my spiritual ears so that I will hear Your voice. I desire to walk under the supernatural anointing of Your Glory!

JACKIE JONES MINISTRIES

Personal Prayer

THE FAST OF ANNA THE PROPHETESS

Luke 2:36-37

³⁶Now there was one, Anna a prophetess, the daughter of Phanuel, of the tribe of Asher. She was of great age, and had lived with a husband seven years from her virginity; ³⁷And this woman was a widow of about eighty-four years, who did not depart from the temple but served God with fasting and prayers night and day.

Anna served God with fasting and praying. She was a servant of the Lord and anointed with the gift of prophecy. Through her fasting and prayers, God spoke to her and anointed her to prophesy of the coming redemption through Jesus Christ. Fasting and praying will open up your heart and spirit to clearly hear from God and empower you to spread the good news of the Kingdom to all.

PRAYER

Lord, I desire to spread the word of God to my family and those around me. I ask for wisdom, knowledge and understanding of Your word and power. Bless me with revelation knowledge and supernatural favor so that I will spread Your gospel to the lost. I pray for wisdom to teach and encourage the brokenhearted and the backslider. Saturate me with Your anointing from heaven so that I will be a voice to the nations and spread the good news of Jesus Christ to all. Bless my mouth so

that the words that I speak will be Your words that will bring forth deliverance and salvation.

Personal Prayer

_____
_____
_____
_____
_____
_____
_____
_____
_____
_____
_____
_____
_____
_____
_____
_____
_____

THE FAST OF ISAIAH

Isaiah 58:6

⁶*"Is this not the fast that I have chosen: To loose the bonds of wickedness, To undo the heavy burdens, To let the oppressed go free, And that you break every yoke?*

In the beginning of Isaiah chapter 58 the wrong reasons for fasting are highlighted. People were fasting for show and continually treated their fellow man with malice in their heart. Isaiah verse 6 reminds us that the fast that is acceptable has to come from the heart to loose the bond of wickedness and heavy burdens. There shall be no wickedness or malice in your heart. Again, we are expected to fast, but we must have the right intention and motive for fasting. Anyone can abstain from food, therefore when fasting we want to touch the heart of God, gain access to the portals of heaven so that blessings can consume us. Therefore fasting must include prayer, meditation and spending time with God!

PRAYER

Lord, I repent now for any malice that is in my heart. Forgive me for selfishness, envy and jealousy against my fellow brother or sister. Forgive me for passing judgment against others. I come humbly before the throne of grace asking for mercy. I pray for freedom from oppression and heavy burdens. I ask for release and

deliverance. I come against depression, oppression and the darts of the enemy. I decree and declare freedom in my life!

Personal Prayer

THE DANIEL FAST

Daniel 1:12

¹²*"Please test your servants for ten days, and let them give us vegetables to eat and water to drink. ¹³Then let our appearance be examined before you, and the appearance of the young men who eat the portion of the king's delicacies; and as you see fit, so deal with your servants." ¹⁴So he consented with them in this matter, and tested them ten days. ¹⁵And at the end of the ten days their features appeared better and fatter in flesh than all the young men who ate the portion of the king's delicacies. ¹⁶Thus the steward took away their portion of delicacies and the wine that they were to drink, and gave them vegetables. As for these four young men, God gave them knowledge and skill in all literature and wisdom; and Daniel had understanding in all visions and dreams.*

The Daniel fast is a very popular fast that can be done corporately and or individually. It is considered a partial fast. Daniel abstained from meat, wine and foods from the king's menu. Instead he chose to just have vegetables and water. Daniel remained steadfast in his faith and love for the one true God. He did not fall prey to the delicacies of his environment. He not only appeared brighter and heathier in his countenance, but he received great wisdom, skill and knowledge. He was also anointed to understand visions and dreams. There is a supernatural anointing in fasting and praying. When you say "**no**" to the flesh and "**yes**" to God, expect to walk in the supernatural favor of God. Daniel walked in God's favor throughout his life and as you read throughout the book of Daniel, he encountered many miracles. Expect to experience the miracles of God when you seek Him and pray.

PRAYER

Lord, I come to the throne of Glory asking for wisdom and a supernatural outpouring of Your favor. Like Daniel, may the favor of blessing rest over my life. May I walk in favor, good health, prosperity, wisdom and power. May the miracles of God's anointing fill me every day of my life. I believe that I shall fulfill the purpose and destiny that has been ordained over my life and the supernatural power of the Holy Spirit will manifest the Glory of God in and around me. The power of the blood of Jesus will cover me, keep me and give me peace.

Personal Prayer

JESUS FASTED

Matthew 4:1-2

¹*Then Jesus was led up by the Spirit into the wilderness to be tempted by the devil.* ²*And when He had fasted forty days and forty nights, afterward He was hungry.*

Jesus also fasted! Jesus walked on earth and gave an example as to how to live our lives, if Jesus Himself fasted, why not us. Strength to stand against the temptations of the devil and the world is imparted when spending time alone with God in prayer and fasting. Moses and Elijah also fasted for 40 days spending time with God. During this time they communed with God and changed the world. You can change the world too!

PRAYER

Lord, shower me with the blessings to be a world changer. Direct my path. Speak to me as I fast and pray and give me the words to share the gospel. As I meditate on Your word, speak to me and order my steps that I may fulfill my purpose. Use me to make a difference and bring others to repentance. I am ready to serve in the Kingdom of God and bring Glory to Your name.

 *Personal Prayer*

_____
_____
_____
_____
_____
_____
_____

Do not get it confused, fasting is not a magic potion; it is a spiritual discipline that is evident throughout the Bible. Although fasting and praying will bring you closer to God, it will not change the will of God. **2 Samuel, chapter 12** tells the story of David's adulterous sin with Bathsheba which resulted in the birth of a child. The child struck ill and although David fasted, the child died on the seventh day. David arose from the fast, washed his face, changed his clothes and entered into the house of the Lord and worshipped the Lord. David accepted the will of God and worshiped God! God is the authority and God's will, will prevail. David's fasting gave him peace and acceptance and drew him closer to God. It is stated in, 2 Samuel, chapter 12 verse 24 that David lays with Bathsheba again, this time as his wife and she bares a son and his name is Solomon. Solomon becomes the wisest man who ever lived and greatly loved by God!

CHAPTER 3
SO WHY FAST AND PRAY

Fasting and praying will open your spiritual eyes and bring you great wisdom. We can all use more wisdom. As it is written in the book of Acts 14:23, Paul and Barnabus fasted for wisdom at the appointment of elders for the churches. Therefore, before you make major decisions, take it to the Lord first and seek his wisdom. Again, a great place to start is in prayer. Before you take that job, before you decide to marry, before you buy that house, or before you sign on the dotted line, pray, fast, seek God first. It is clearly stated in Proverbs 3:6, "In all your ways acknowledge Him, and He shall direct your paths."

I do not want to make any decisions without seeking God's guidance first. I need Godly wisdom every day. That should be a daily prayer. Lord, fill me with wisdom today and every day. There are distractions everywhere and we can easily step into the wrong path or eat from the wrong tree if we are not alert and walking with Christ. This is why it is so important to pray always.

Through Fasting and praying you develop a stronger relationship with God. Welcome the love and guidance of the Holy Spirit who will give you wisdom and understanding in your daily walk. Read carefully and heed to this plea, God is calling us to humble ourselves in prayer and turn from all wicked ways. You do not want to live your life outside of the presence of God.

God loves you and wants to commune with you. It is so awesome to live a life filled with the Spirit of the living God. So why fast and pray? I can't imagine life without a close walk with God. I need God's wisdom, guidance and direction. I need to walk and live in God's presence and spending time fasting and praying will open the portals of heaven so that I can experience everything that God has for me!

A fast can be absolute or partial. A fast can be for 1 day, 3 days, 10 days or 40 days. A fast can be all day or just a meal a day. A fast can be for repentance, deliverance, intercession, clarity, wisdom, direction, strength and supernatural favor and power. Reading your Bible, meditating and praying are the essential components of fasting. Fasting can change your life and your situation. We become more aware of God's provision. We become more aware of our dependency on God.

I often use the term ***"put yourself in time out"*** as a means to find a quiet area, with no television, telephone or distractions, so that you can spend time with God. Just you and God! Create an atmosphere where you can commune with God and allow yourself to enter into His gates with thanksgiving and into His courts with praise and see the Glory of God's manifested power and love surround you. You can use soft worship music to set the atmosphere of abiding and abide in His love. As you pray, the heavenly portals will open up and the supernatural blessing will flow!

Fasting and praying will definitely give you clarity and insight. Fasting and praying will certainly put you in position to walk freely with God and to receive all that God has for you to live abundantly blessed. Expect to see results when you spend time with God in prayer and fasting. We are living in a season and a world where spending time with God is pertinent to your journey. I encourage you to make the time to fast and pray. Trust me, make the time to fast and pray and you will live the results of answered prayer and supernatural favor.

CHAPTER 4
THE POWER OF PRAYING THE WORD OF GOD

There is so much power in prayer and praying the Word of God brings life and freedom. Jesus gave us a great example of using the Word of God. When He was tempted in the wilderness by the devil (Matthew 4:1-11), Jesus quoted from the Word of God each time. The Power that came forth from the Word of God was victorious over the tricks and temptation of the enemy. When we pray the Word of God, we tell God what He says in His Word!

There are prayers throughout the Bible. We can pray from the book of Psalms, Proverbs, Prophets, and my personal favorite is praying the Promises of God. I love to recite in my prayer time the promises that are written throughout the Bible. The Bible is full of promises.

I will randomly share just a few of God's promises that you can pray just to get you started.

Genesis 22:18; In your seed all the nations of the earth shall be blessed. Because you have obeyed my voice.

Exodus 14:14; The Lord will fight for you. And you shall hold your peace

Exodus 33:14; *My presence will go with you, and I will give you rest.*

Numbers 6:24-26; *The Lord bless you and keep you; 25. The Lord make His face shine upon you, And be gracious to you, 26. The Lord lift up His countenance upon you, And give you peace.*

Deuteronomy 20:4; *For the Lord your God is He who goes with you, to fight for you against your enemies, to save you.*

Isaiah 40:31; *But those who wait on the Lord shall renew their strength; They shall mount up with wings like eagles, they shall run and not be weary, They shall walk and not faint.*

Isaiah 54:17; *No weapon formed against you shall prosper, and every tongue which rises against you in judgment you shall not condemn. This is the heritage of the servants of the Lord.*

Joshua 1:9; *Be strong and of good courage; do not be afraid, nor dismayed for the Lord your God is with you wherever you go.*

II Samuel 22:4; *I will call upon the Lord who is worthy to be praised; So shall I be saved from my enemies*

I Chronicles 4:10; *And Jabez called on the God of Israel saying, Oh, that You would bless me indeed, and enlarge* *my territory, that Your hand would be with me, and that you would keep me from evil, that I may not cause pain! So God granted him what he requested.*

II Chronicles 15:7; *But you, be strong and do not let your hands be weak, for your work shall be rewarded.*

Job 10:12; *You have granted me life and favor, And Your care has preserved my spirit.*

Psalms 1:1-3; *Blessed is the man Who walks not in the counsel of the ungodly, Nor stands in the path of sinners, Nor sits in the seat of the scornful; 2. But his delight is in the law of the Lord, And he meditates day and night. 3. He shall shall be like a tree planted by the rivers of water, That brings forth its fruit in its season, whose leaf also shall not wither; And whatever he does shall prosper.*

Psalms 9: 9-10; *The Lord will be a refuge for the oppressed, A refuge in times of trouble. 10. And those who know Your name will put their trust in You; For You, Lord have not forsaken those who seek You.*

Jeremiah 29:11; *For I know the thoughts I think towards you says the Lord, thoughts of peace and not evil, to give you a future and a hope.*

Psalms 84:11; *For the Lord God is a sun and shield; The Lord will give grace and glory; No good thing will He withhold*

Psalms 91:4-6; *He shall cover you with His feathers, and under His wings you shall take refuge; His truth shall be your shield and buckler. 5. You shall not be afraid of the terror by night, nor of the arrow that flies by day, 6. Nor of the pestilence that walks in darkness, Nor of the destruction that lays waste at noonday.*

Psalms 103:2-3; *Bless the Lord, O my soul, and forget not all His benefits: 3. Who forgives all your iniquities, Who heals all your diseases.*

Proverbs 3:5-6; *Trust in the Lord with all your heart, and lean not on your own understanding; 6. In all your ways acknowledge Him, And he shall direct your paths.*

Proverbs 18:10; *The name of the Lord is a strong tower; The righteous run to it and are safe.*

Philippians 4:19; *And my God shall supply all your needs according to His riches in glory by Christ Jesus*

Jeremiah 30:17; *For I will restore health to you, And heal you of your wounds, says the Lord*

John 15:27; *Peace I give to you not as the world gives do I give to you. Let not your heart be troubled, neither let it be afraid.*

Mark 11:24; *Therefore, I say to you, whatever things you ask when you pray, believe that you receive them, and you will have them.*

Luke 11:9-10; *So I say to you, ask, and it will be given to you; seek, and you will find; knock, and it will be opened to you. 10. For everyone who asks receives, and he who seeks finds, and to him who knocks it will be opened.*

John 11:25-26; *Jesus said, I am the resurrection and the life. He who believes in Me, though he may die, he shall live. 26. And whoever lives and believes in Me shall never die.*

Romans 8:28-29; *And we know that all things work together for good to those who love God, to those who are called according to His purpose. 29. For who He foreknew, He also predestined to be conformed to the image of His Son, that He might be the firstborn among many brethren.*

II Corinthians 5:17; *Therefore, if anyone is in Christ, he is a new creation; old things have passed away; behold, all things have become new.*

Galatians 3:13-14; *Christ has redeemed us from the curse of the law, having become a curse for us (for it is written, "Cursed is everyone who hangs on a tree"), 14. that the blessings of Abraham might come upon the Gentiles in*

Christ Jesus, that we might receive the promise of the Spirit through faith.

Ephesians 1:3; *Blessed be the God and Father of our Lord Jesus Christ, who has blessed us with every spiritual blessing in heavenly places.*

Ephesians 3:20; *Now to Him who is able to do exceedingly abundantly above all that we ask or think, according to the power that works in us.*

Philippians 1:6; *being confident of this very thing, that He who has begun a good work in you will complete it until the day of Jesus Christ.*

Philippians 4:19; *And my God shall supply all your need according to His riches in glory by Christ Jesus.*

Colossians 1:12-14; *giving thanks to the Father who has qualified us to be partakers of the inheritance of the saints in the light. 13. He has delivered us from the power of darkness and conveyed us into the kingdom of the Son of His love, 14. In whom we have redemption through His blood, the forgiveness of sins.*

I Timothy 1:14; *And the grace of our Lord was exceedingly abundant, with faith and love which are in Christ Jesus.*

James 5:14-15; *Is anyone among you sick? Let them call the elders of the church to pray over them and anoint them* *with oil in the name of the Lord. 15. And the prayer of faith will save the sick, the Lord will raise them up. And if he has committed sins, he will be forgiven.*

Philippians 4:13; *I can do all things through Jesus Christ who strengthens me.*

I challenge you to integrate these promises into your prayers. Recite them out loud and watch the power of God move over your life and circumstances. Trust and believe and you will experience the awesomeness of God through prayer!

CHAPTER 5
PRAYING AND BELIEVING

We can fast and pray, but without believing we negate the prayer. We must have faith! Now faith is the substance of things hoped for, the evidence of things not seen (*Hebrews 11:1*). We must believe what we are praying for before we see the manifestation.

One of my most favorite stories in the Bible is the story of the woman with the issue of blood. It is a great demonstration of faith (*Luke 8:43-48*). A woman had a flow of blood or her menstruation for twelve years. According to Leviticus 15:19-30, a woman on her menstruation was ceremonially unclean, therefore everyone or everything that she touched became unclean. She must have been an outcast and most likely lived alone. She spent all of her money on doctors and still could not be healed. She heard about Jesus. She had faith to believe if she can just touch the hem of his clothing, she would receive her healing. She made her way through the crowd and reached out and touched his clothing and she was immediately healed. In the midst of the crowd, Jesus perceived power flow out of him and asked "Who touched me?" The woman fell before him and in the presence of the crowd shared the reason she touched him and shared that she was immediately healed. Jesus said her faith made her well! It was her faith that made her venture out of her place of loneliness, depression and illness. It was her faith that made her walk through a crowd of people ignoring the belittling looks, the awful words and the uncanny stares. But she believed that if she could just touch the hem of his garment she would be healed. Her faith made her well.

Throughout the bible we will find many stories of faith. Faith is believing the impossible. The woman with the issue of blood reached out and touched the hem of Jesus' garment. She touched the heart of Jesus. We must touch the heart of Jesus in our prayers. When you pray, you must believe! Believing prayers will touch the heart of God. Mark 11:24 says "Therefore, I say unto you, whatsoever things you ask when you pray, believe that you receive them, and you will have them". It is also written in Matthew 21:22, "Whatever things you ask in prayer, believing, you will receive."

Someone may say, I don't have a lot of faith. But it is written in Matthew 17:20 "If you have faith as a mustard seed, you can say to this mountain, "Move from here to there" and it will move and nothing will be impossible for you." Just a little faith can move mountains. So keep praying and keep believing. As I am writing this paragraph, I am praying for a young man by the name of Omari who is currently in surgery. I am believing God for a miracle!

The more you pray, the more you will desire to pray and the closer you will get to God! Praying will give you power, strength and an open door to the kingdom of God! Fasting, Praying and Believing will CHANGE YOUR LIFE!

By the way, I am adding this sentence as I send this to the publisher, Omari made it through surgery victoriously!!!!! Prayer works! Carry it everywhere you go and watch the supernatural move of God show up!!!!

I would love to hear the testimonies of your fasting experience.

Email me at:
revjackiejones@aol.com

BE BLESSED AND FAVORED!

www.JackieJonesMinistries.org

ABOUT THE AUTHOR

Jackie Jones has been an associate minister for almost 3 decades at the Mount Moriah A.M.E. Church in Cambria Heights, Queens. Her spiritual insight into the heart of women and men have touched and changed lives everywhere. Jackie Jones has a monthly women's fellowship; where the women meet in an intimate atmosphere to discover biblical answers to everyday issues. Her passion is to help people reach their fullest potential and discover their purpose in life.

Jackie Jones is an inspirational speaker that uplifts and encourages women and men to live healthy and holy lives spiritually, emotionally and physically. She is a walking vessel for God that demonstrates a life of holiness is a life of abundant blessing.

Jackie Jones also has a desire to have young men and women recognize their potential and God given gifts. As such, she also ministers through her profession as a New York City Principal working with the Special Education population and specializing in the behavior problems of our youth. She believes that nothing is impossible for God and spreads the goodness of Jesus in all that she does.

Jackie Jones has a Bachelor of Arts in Psychology, a Master of Science in Special Education, a Master of Science in Leadership and Administration and is presently completing a dissertation for her Doctorate Degree in Educational Leadership. She is a strong advocate in the education field.

Jackie Jones is happily married with 3 beautiful children. Although she is called to work in the ministry, she thanks God daily for her first ministry and that is her family.

Jackie Jones lives by the scripture, Philippians 4:13 "I can do all things through Jesus Christ who strengthens me"!